Hello, Beautiful!

Backyard Animals

WORLD
BOOK

www.worldbook.com

World Book, Inc.
180 North LaSalle Street, Suite 900
Chicago, Illinois 60601
USA

For information about other World Book
publications, visit our website at
www.worldbook.com or call
1-800-WORLDBK (967-5325).

For information about sales to schools and
libraries, call 1-800-975-3250 (United States),
or 1-800-837-5365 (Canada).

Library of Congress Cataloging-in-Publication
Data for this volume has been applied for.

Hello, Beautiful!
ISBN: 978-0-7166-3567-3 (set, hc.)

Backyard Animals
ISBN: 978-0-7166-3568-0 (hc.)

Also available as:
ISBN: 978-0-7166-3578-9 (e-book)

Printed in China by Shenzhen Wing King Tong
Paper Products Co., Ltd., Shenzhen, Guangdong
1st printing July 2018

Staff

Writer: Grace Guibert

Executive Committee

President
Jim O'Rourke

Vice President and
Editor in Chief
Paul A. Kobasa

Vice President, Finance
Donald D. Keller

Vice President, Marketing
Jean Lin

Vice President,
International Sales
Maksim Rutenberg

Vice President, Technology
Jason Dole

Director, Human Resources
Bev Ecker

Editorial

Director, New Print
Tom Evans

Managing Editor, New Print
Jeff De La Rosa

Senior Editor, New Print
Shawn Brennan

Editor, New Print
Grace Guibert

Librarian
S. Thomas Richardson

Manager, Contracts &
Compliance (Rights &
Permissions)
Loranne K. Shields

Manager, Indexing Services
David Pofelski

Digital

Director, Digital Content
Development
Emily Kline

Director, Digital Product
Development
Erika Meller

Manager, Digital Products
Jonathan Wills

Graphics and Design

Senior Art Director
Tom Evans

Senior Visual
Communications Designer
Melanie Bender

Media Researcher
Rosalia Bledsoe

Manufacturing/
Production

Manufacturing Manager
Anne Fritzinger

Proofreader
Nathalie Strassheim

Photographic credits:

Cover: © Shutterstock.

© Rick & Nora Bowers, Alamy Images 16-17; © Shutterstock 4, 6-15, 18-29.

Contents

Introduction

Welcome to "Hello, Beautiful!" picture books!

This book is about animals you might see in your backyard. Each book in the "Hello, Beautiful!" series uses large, colorful photographs and a few words to describe our world to children who are not yet reading on their own or are beginning to learn to read. For the benefit of both grown-up and child readers, a picture key is included in the back of the volume to describe each photograph and specific type of animal in more detail.

"Hello, Beautiful!" books can help pre-readers and starting readers get into the habit of having fun with books and learning from them, too. With pre-readers, a grown-up reader (parent, grandparent, librarian, teacher, older brother or sister) can point to the words on each page as he or she speaks them aloud to help the listening child associate the concept of text with the object or idea it describes.

Large, colorful photographs give pre-readers plenty to see while they listen to the reader. If no reader is available, pre-readers can "read" on their own, turning the pages of the book and speaking their own stories about what they see. For new readers, the photographs provide visual hints about the words on the page. Often, these words describe the specific type of animal shown. This animal may not be representative of all species, or types, of that animal.

This book displays some of the animals that climb, crawl, dig, fly, hop, or prance into backyards around the world. These are animals children are likely to encounter. Help inspire respect and care for these important and beautiful animals by sharing this "Hello, Beautiful!" book with a child soon.

Butterfly

Hello, beautiful butterfly!

You are a silver-washed fritillary butterfly. You fly from flower to flower! Your orange-and-black wings flash in the sunlight.

Your short front legs help you find food to eat.

Deer

Hello, beautiful deer!

You are a **red** deer. You roam around forests and sometimes into backyards!

Male deer like you grow large, bony antlers on top of your head. Antlers look like tree branches.

Dragonfly

Hello, beautiful dragonfly!

You are a green darner dragonfly. You have four wings, big eyes, and a colorful body.

You can hang in the air like a helicopter!

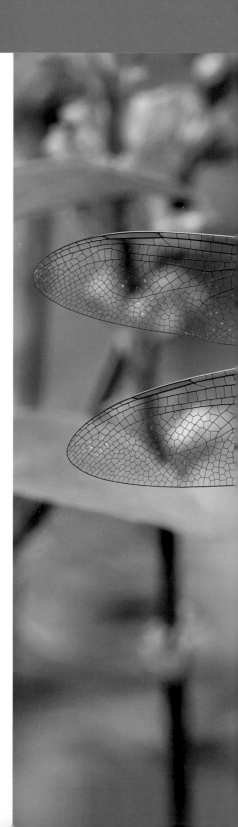

Earthworm

Hello, beautiful earthworm!

You are a night crawler earthworm. You crawl through the soil looking for food.

You do not have eyes or ears, but you have five pairs of hearts! ♥

Frog

Hello, beautiful frog!

You are an American bullfrog. You live near the water. You are a great swimmer.

You have long back
legs that help you
j u m p!

Gecko

Hello, beautiful gecko!

You are a western banded gecko. You are covered with bumpy scales.

If your tail breaks off, you can grow a new one!

Owl

Hello, beautiful owl!

You are a barn owl. You have big, round eyes. They help you see well when you hunt.

You sleep during the day and stay awake at night.

Pigeon

Hello, beautiful pigeon!

You are a rock pigeon.
You are a kind of pigeon
that lives in big cities.

You are a strong bird.
You can fly fast and high.

Possum

Hello, beautiful possum!

You are a brush-tailed possum.

You have a bushy tail and pointed ears.

You are a great climber!
Your feet can hold on tightly
to tree branches.

Rabbit

Hello, beautiful rabbit!

You are a European rabbit.
You hOP, hOP, hOP
through the yard
on your hind legs!

Your fluffy tail
looks like a ball
of cotton.

Skunk

Hello, beautiful skunk!

You are a striped skunk.
You are **black** with white
stripes down your back
and tail.

We do not like you in our
backyard! When you are
scared, you spray out
something that smells awful!

Squirrel

Hello, beautiful squirrel!

You are an eastern gray squirrel. You have a bushy tail and sharp front teeth.

Your claws help you scurry up trees and leap from branch to branch!

Picture Key

Find out more about these backyard animals! Use the picture keys below to learn where each animal lives, how big it grows, and its favorite foods!

Butterfly

Hello, beautiful butterfly!

You are a silver-washed fritillary butterfly. You fly from flower to flower! Your orange-and-black wings flash in the sunlight.

Your short front legs help you find food to eat.

Deer

Hello, beautiful deer!

You are a red deer. You roam around forests and sometimes into backyards!

Male deer like you grow large, bony antlers on top of your head. Antlers look like tree branches.

Dragonfly

Hello, beautiful dragonfly!

You are a green darner dragonfly. You have four wings, big eyes, and a colorful body.

You can hang in the air like a helicopter!

Pages 6-7 Butterfly
The silver-washed fritillary *(FRIHT uh LEHR ee)* lives throughout much of Europe and Asia. Its wingspread is about 2 ½ inches (6 centimeters). It often feeds on the *nectar* (sweet juice) from flowers from bramble plants, shrubs, or vines with prickly stems.

Pages 8-9 Deer
The red deer lives in the forests of Europe, Asia, and northern Africa. A *hart* (adult male) weighs from 250 to 350 pounds (113 to 159 kilograms) and stands 3 ½ to 4 ½ feet (1 to 1.4 meters) tall. Deer eat a variety of plants, including grasses, flowers, twigs, leaves, branches, and bark.

Pages 10-11 Dragonfly
The green darner dragonfly is a common dragonfly of North America. It is also found in Central America, Bermuda, and some Caribbean Islands. They measure about 3 inches (8 centimeters) in both length and wingspread. Dragonflies eat mostly other flying insects.

Earthworm

Hello, beautiful earthworm!

You are a night crawler earthworm. You crawl through the soil looking for food.

You do not have eyes or ears, but you have five pairs of hearts! ▼

Frog

Hello, beautiful frog!

You are an American bullfrog. You live near the water. You are a great swimmer.

You have long back legs that help you j u m p!

Gecko

Hello, beautiful gecko!

You are a western banded gecko. You are covered with bumpy scales.

If your tail breaks off, you can grow a new one!

Pages 12-13 Earthworm
Night crawler earthworms can be found in moist, warm soil throughout the world. These worms range in size from ¹/₂₅ inch (1 millimeter) to 11 feet (3 meters) long. They feed on dead plant material that is found in the soil.

Pages 14-15 Frog
The American bullfrog lives in most parts of North America east of the Rocky Mountains and in many parts of the west. It grows about 8 inches (20 centimeters) long, not including its hind legs, which may stretch 10 inches (25 centimeters) long. Bullfrogs eat insects and other small animals.

Pages 16-17 Gecko
The western banded gecko *(GEHK oh)* can be found in the southwestern United States and northern Mexico. Western banded geckos grow up to 6 inches (15 centimeters) in length, including their tail. Banded geckos eat small insects, spiders, and even baby scorpions.

Owl

Hello, beautiful owl!

You are a barn owl. You have big, round eyes. They help you see well when you hunt.

You sleep during the day and stay awake at night.

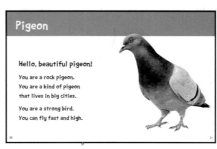

Pigeon

Hello, beautiful pigeon!

You are a rock pigeon. You are a kind of pigeon that lives in big cities.

You are a strong bird. You can fly fast and high.

Possum

Hello, beautiful possum!

You are a brush-tailed possum.

You have a bushy tail and pointed ears.

You are a great climber! Your feet can hold on tightly to tree branches.

Pages 18-19 Owl

Barn owls live in *temperate* (moderate) and warm climates worldwide. They measure about 15 to 16 inches (38 to 41 centimeters) long and have a wingspread of 40 to 44 inches (100 to 110 centimeters). Barn owls eat mainly such small rodents as mice, rats, and voles. Occasionally, they also eat birds, insects, and small reptiles and amphibians.

Pages 20-21 Pigeon

The rock pigeon is native to cliffs in Africa, Asia, and Europe. Today, it is a common sight in cities around the world. It measures from 10 to 15 inches (25 to 38 centimeters) long. In cities, rock pigeons can live on scraps of human food like bread and popcorn. In more rural settings, rock pigeons search for seeds, berries, and acorns.

Pages 22-23 Possum

The brush-tailed possum lives in Australian cities. Adults weigh from 3 to 11 pounds (1.4 to 5 kilograms). These possums raid fruit trees and garbage cans for food. They move about at night and sleep during the day.

Rabbit

Hello, beautiful rabbit!

You are a European rabbit. You h o P, h o P, h o P through the yard on your hind legs!

Your fluffy tail looks like a ball of cotton.

Skunk

Hello, beautiful skunk!

You are a striped skunk. You are **black with white** stripes down your back and tail.

We do not like you in our backyard! When you are scared, you spray out something that smells awful!

Squirrel

Hello, beautiful squirrel!

You are an eastern gray squirrel. You have a bushy tail and sharp front teeth.

Your claws help you scurry up trees and leap from branch to branch!

Pages 24-25 Rabbit

The European rabbit originally lived in southern Europe and northern Africa, and on some western Mediterranean islands. Today, they are among the most widespread rabbits. European rabbits are from 15 to 20 inches (38 to 50 centimeters) long and weigh between 3 $\frac{1}{3}$ and 5 $\frac{1}{2}$ pounds (1.5 and 2.5 kilograms). Rabbits eat green leafy plants, including clover, grass, and herbs. When these are sparse, they eat twigs, bark, and fruit.

Pages 26-27 Skunk

The striped skunk is the most common species of skunk in the United States. It also lives in Canada and in northern Mexico. Striped skunks grow from 13 to 18 inches (33 to 46 centimeters) long, not including the tail, and weigh from 3 to 10 pounds (1.4 to 4.5 kilograms). Skunks eat caterpillars and such insects as beetles, crickets, and grasshoppers. They also eat mice, rats, and other small rodents. Sometimes they eat eggs, fruit, grain, and the rotting remains of dead animals.

Pages 28-29 Squirrel

The eastern gray squirrel is native to the eastern United States and Canada. It ranges in size from 15 to 21 inches (38 to 53 centimeters) long, including the tail, which is about 6 to 10 inches (15 to 25 centimeters) long. Like other squirrels, they eat seeds, nuts, and parts of trees.

Index